ESPECIALLY FOR

....

WITH LOVE FROM

....

ONE
PERFECT PLAN

THE BIBLE'S BIG STORY IN TINY POEMS

WRITTEN BY **NANCY TUPPER LING**

WATERBROOK

ILLUSTRATED BY **ALINA CHAU**

One word—

then light breaks into darkness;
the sky, the seas, and life—how wondrous!

....

Read more about **CREATION** *in Genesis 1.*

One garden—
here's Eden, where God's creatures roam;
see Adam and Eve in their glorious home.

One serpent—
he says, "You surely won't die."
A bite of the fruit reveals
Satan's lie.

One world—
now broken as sin enters in.
How will our Father restore
it again?

One God—
whose plan is perfect and true—
will bring new life to me and to you.

Read more about **THE GARDEN OF EDEN** and **THE FALL** in
Genesis 2:8–25; 3:1–7, 22–24.

One drop—

then two; water floods the land.
When the rain stops, God's promise still stands.

....

Read more about **THE FLOOD** *and* **THE RAINBOW COVENANT** *in Genesis 7:4–10; 9:11–13.*

One couple—

they pray for a child to love;
God gives them more than the stars above.

Read more about **ABRAHAM AND SARAH** in Genesis 15:1–6; 21:1–3.

One coat—

Joseph's dreams are not understood;

what his brothers mean for evil, God means for good.

Read more about **JOSEPH** in Genesis 37:3–11; 50:15–20.

One cry to God—
soon Israel will see
Moses return to set them free.
Out from bondage, a people redeemed,
led by fire and clouds to a land of their dreams.

One God—
our Savior, Redeemer, and Friend—
loves all children from now till the end.

Read more about **ISRAEL'S DELIVERANCE** in Exodus 6.6–8.

One promise—

then Ruth with Naomi remains:

"Your God is my God for all of my days."

....

Read more about **RUTH** *in Ruth 1:6–16.*

One stone—
sets sail from David's strong sling;
Goliath soon falls to a shepherd turned king.

Read more about **DAVID** in 1 Samuel 17:1–50.

One queen—
emboldened by God to be brave
for a time such as this;
her people are saved.

Read more about **ESTHER** *in Esther 4:14; 8:3–6.*

One king—

throws Daniel into a den.
God saves His servant from every lion.

Read more about **DANIEL** *in Daniel 6:1–23.*

One big fish—

it swallows Jonah alive!

Three days in this tomb, and still he survives.

*Read more about **JONAH** in Jonah 1–2.*

One God—

our Savior, Redeemer,
and Friend;
throughout all time,
God protects and
defends.

One angel—
appears to the Virgin Mary:
"A Savior comes, whom you shall carry."

Read more about **THE FORETELLING OF JESUS'S BIRTH** *in Luke 1:26–33.*

One heavenly light—
one humble stable;
shepherds make haste to our Lord's cradle.

Read more about **JESUS'S BIRTH** *in Luke 2:6–18.*

One child—

Jesus grows into a man,
God's precious gift and salvation plan.

Read more about **JESUS'S CHILDHOOD** in Luke 2:22–52.

Two fish—

yes, two, plus five loaves of bread;
Christ feeds the masses as word of Him spreads.

Read more about **THE FEEDING OF THE FIVE THOUSAND** *in John 6:1–11.*

One touch—

Christ commands, "Little girl, arise!"
Then Jairus's daughter opens her eyes.

Read more about **JAIRUS'S DAUGHTER** *in Mark 5:22–24, 35–43.*

One leper—

returns, though Jesus healed ten;
his faith makes him whole, washed spotless again.
Jesus heals the lame, calms the raging seas,
gives sight to the blind, sets the captives free.

Read more about **JESUS'S MIRACLES** *in Matthew 9:1–8; Mark 4:35–41; 5:1–20; Luke 17:11–19; John 9:1–7.*

One God—
our Savior, Redeemer, and Friend,
Alpha, Omega, Beginning, and End.

One donkey—
it carries Jesus to town;
people spread cloaks and
palms on the ground.

Read more about **JESUS'S TRIUMPHAL ENTRY**
in Matthew 21:1–9.

One cross—

the crowds now shout, "Crucify!"

For you and me, He was willing to die.

Read more about **JESUS'S CRUCIFIXION** *in John 19:16–30.*

One empty tomb—
the stone's rolled away.
Rejoice! Rejoice! Christ is risen today!

Read more about **JESUS'S RESURRECTION** *in Mark 16:1–8.*

One Holy Spirit—

like wind descends;

with new believers, Christ's kingdom expands.

God calls us still to show the Way

so all will hear this Good News someday.

Read more about **THE GREAT COMMISSION** *and* **PENTECOST**
in Matthew 28:16–20; Acts 2:1–33.

One heaven on earth—

where we will dwell.

Every tear's wiped away, and all will be well!

One God—
our God, so perfect and true—
has offered new life to me
and to you.

Read more about **GOD'S KINGDOM** *in Revelation 21:1–4.*

ONE PERFECT PLAN

Text copyright © 2023 by Nancy Tupper Ling
Cover art and interior illustrations copyright © 2023 by Alina Hiu-Fan Chau

Published in the United States by WaterBrook,
an imprint of Random House,
a division of Penguin Random House LLC.

WATERBROOK and colophon are registered trademarks
of Penguin Random House LLC.

ISBN 978-0-593-57939-8
Ebook ISBN 978-0-593-57940-4

The Library of Congress catalog record is available at https://lccn.loc.gov/2022013220.

Printed in China

waterbrookmultnomah.com

10 9 8 7 6 5 4 3 2 1

First Edition

Book and cover design by Nina Simoneaux

SPECIAL SALES Most WaterBrook books are available at special quantity discounts when
purchased in bulk by corporations, organizations, and special-interest groups. Custom
imprinting or excerpting can also be done to fit special needs. For information, please
email specialmarketscms@penguinrandomhouse.com.

For my mom—
who instilled in me a love
of words and the Word.
Soli Deo gloria.

—NANCY

For those who guide and encourage
me when my faith wavers and who love
and support me along my journey.

—ALINA

NANCY TUPPER LING is a children's author, poet, bookseller, and librarian. Basically, she surrounds herself with books! Occasionally she creates a few books of her own, including this one, plus *The Story I'll Tell, Double Happiness, The Yin-Yang Sisters,* and *For Every Little Thing* with co-author, June Cotner. Visit her website to learn more: www.nancytupperling.com.